To Mark —
Thank you again
for your inspiring
words! I hope you enjoy
the stories. Keep moving forward!
Blessings,
Annie Martin
6/17/22

D0984518

The Art of Picking Up Dog Poop

Leading from the Middle

BY CONNIE MARTIN

Copyright © 2021 by Constance G. Martin

All rights reserved. No part of this publication may be reproduced, distributed or transmitted in any form or by any means, including photocopying, recording, or other electronic or mechanical methods, without the prior written permission of the publisher, except in the case of brief quotations embodied in critical reviews and certain other noncommercial uses permitted by copyright law.

For permission requests, write to the publisher, addressed "Attention: Permissions Coordinator," at the address below.

Published by: HigherLife Publishing & Marketing
PO Box 623307
Oviedo, FL 32762
www.ahigherlife.com

Cover Illustrations by Mark Herron
Photography by Dale R. Deaton
Typesetting by Jonathan Lewis

The Art of Picking Up Dog Poop / Constance G. Martin -- 1st ed.
ISBN 978-1-951492-26-7 Hardback
ISBN 978-1-951492-27-4 eBook

Printed in the United States of America.
10 9 8 7 6 5 4 3 2 1

This book is dedicated to my past, present, and future generations.

Contents

Preface

Leading from the Middle

Why write about picking up dog poop? How does that process relate to overcoming setbacks, navigating change, and leading from the middle of an organization? Read on, and I will give you the *poop* on both.

After twenty years in Colorado, I moved across the country with my two adult dogs in the middle of June. Yes, I took my energetic furry friends out of their large backyard in beautiful Colorado Springs on a four-day road trip, with many new adventures, across this great country to Central Florida.

To set the stage, the house in Colorado stood at the front of a thirteen-thousand-square-foot lot at the top of a cul-de-sac, with most of the property in the backyard sitting on a slight hill. Three mature cottonwood trees lined the fence and provided shade in the summer as the dogs enjoyed chasing the squirrels. The ground stayed frozen for much of the winter, and it was often too cold to do yard maintenance. Depending on the weather, I could easily go a couple of months without picking up the poop. The grass would go dormant in October and come back to life in late April as the snow turned to rain or hail. I recall standing in the middle of the yard with my rake and shovel, surveying the dead grass and leaves combined with the poop scattered throughout the yard. I would put on my headphones or bring the radio out and start raking. I'd rake the leaves and poop into piles and then, with the big snow shovel, scoop them up and dump them into a lawn bag (with gloves on, of course!).

I should clarify: this chore could take a couple of hours to complete. As I made my way diligently across the yard in the welcome sunshine, my mind would wander through many topics in no particular order.

I would think about something someone said the day before, what I might do differently the next time in a particular situation, or how I couldn't pawn off a particular unpleasant task on someone else.

At times, I've had similar thoughts in my work and leadership experiences. Yes, I'm relating leadership experiences to picking up dog poop! I've occasionally shared some of my stories during watercooler chats—which many of my colleagues, some fellow dog owners, could relate to—and then found my coworkers and I could relate many of the funny poop stories to practical situations in the workplace. For example, transitioning into a new job, you may find yourself picking up a bit of "poop" from your predecessor. As information flows quickly from your predecessor, often noted as "drinking from a fire hose," it may feel just as overwhelming as looking across the big backyard after hours of cleanup to see several more piles that still need to be picked up. After a few weeks of drinking from a fire hose as the new lead, the first time you finish that key team meeting and realize the team has accepted you as the lead brings a feeling of satisfaction similar to the one you would have at the end of a picking-up-poop chore when you can finally cross that chore off your list.

With twenty-five years in the corporate world mentoring young leaders and being mentored by some of the best as well, my hope is to impart some of the nuggets of wisdom I've *picked up* along the way in my unique and diverse life.

Over the years, I have also found that leading from the middle exercises some of the same contradictions found in the paradox of the middle child. As a middle child in my family, I have an older brother, a younger sister, a younger stepsister, and two younger stepbrothers. One of the best descriptions of the middle child— which really resonates with me—comes from *The Birth Order Book: Why You Are the Way You Are* by Dr. Kevin Leman:

> I've looked at many charts listing characteristics of middleborn children and found them to be an exercise in paradox. An example of one of these charts appears below, containing two columns with words and phrases that can all be very typical of the middle child. The left- and right-hand columns have been arranged to illustrate some of the direct contradictions you can find in this birth order:

The Middleborn: Inconsistent Paradox

Loner, quiet, shy	Sociable, friendly, outgoing
Impatient, easily frustrated	Takes life in stride, laid-back
Very competitive	Easygoing, not competitive
Rebel, family goat	Peacemaker, mediator
Aggressive, a scrapper	Avoids conflict

The bottom line is that the middle child is "iffy"—the product of many pressures coming from different directions. More than any other birth order, you must look at the entire family to understand a particular middle child. How he or she finally turns out is about as predictable as a Chicago weather report. In many ways, the middle child remains a mystery."[1]

In the pages that follow, I combine entertaining stories with practical tips for leaders in the middle to overcome setbacks, navigate challenges, and thrive in the workplace. I have found that we all have something unique to bring to the conversation. You may see me blend stories from different times in my life: when I was a swimmer, a lifeguard, a US Army lieutenant, a wife, a working mother of two, an ex-wife, a software lead in corporate America, and, of course, a dog owner. My hope is that my life experiences will not only empower and grow your leadership style in your workplace as well as other areas of your life but also have you giggling the way my colleagues and I did when I first shared them.

Introduction

Enjoy the Journey!

Have you ever taken a short flight or road trip and found yourself sitting next to someone who entertains you with her stories? I wrote this book with that experience in mind. Imagine yourself on a trip with a mentor you may have always wanted to know a little better, who is sharing both highlights and tough days from her life while imparting wisdom and lessons learned—and making you chuckle.

In this longer-than-usual conversation, I would like to invite you to come along on my journey for a while. I share personal stories with the intent to give you practical tips, make you smile, and help you see your situation from a new perspective.

Some of the stories will surprise you, such as picking up poop off the bottom of a pool. Others will ask you tough questions or remind you of difficult seasons. However, I have learned that in the retelling of the story, in the reminiscing, we not only find healing ourselves but also help others heal in the process.

Each chapter reveals a different experience of mine that I relate to some aspect of picking up dog poop. And each chapter contains a leadership nugget (or more) for you to *pick up*—practical advice you can implement in your own workplace and life as well as share with others.

Whether you feel stuck in the middle of some of your worst days, surrounded by dog poop, or are looking for some practical ways to manage change and transition, there is something in this book for you—to help you find a way to pick up the pieces and start thriving again. Fasten your seat belt and enjoy the journey!

–1–

Seriously?

Keep a Sense of Humor

He handed me two small specimen cups and said, "Take these and bring back samples next week."

"Seriously?" I asked with a smile and a raised eyebrow.

"Yes, if you can get them. First thing in the morning would be best," he responded. Both dogs looked at me expectantly, excited to go on the car ride back to the house. Cody, my oldest dog, was a sixty-five-pound black shepherd-Lab mix with fluffy fur like a teddy bear, tall ears, and a white spot on his chest and his two front paws. He would wag his half-sized fluffy tail often. Dingo, who was about six months younger than Cody, was a black-and-gray purebred blue heeler with a soft, short coat and a stocky chest, and about the same weight as Cody. His tan legs were lightning fast, and his long tail acted as a rudder as he zoomed and circled around. Both of these beautiful animals seemed to talk and provided daily amusement.

So there I was on a fall Saturday morning in Colorado with Pikes Peak at my back, all decked out in my sweats and boat shoes before breakfast and coffee. The vet had suggested the dogs would be more cooperative first thing in the morning, so I decided to don my tools for the collection process. Since I didn't have gloves handy, I improvised and covered both hands with plastic shopping bags from the local supermarket. I picked up two large red plastic cups, each labeled with a dog's name, and finally opened the door for dogs that had waited not so patiently for the early morning business. I recall thinking, "Thank goodness no pictures exist for this getup."

I started with Cody since he tended to mark just about everything in sight. Cody gave me a curious look as I followed him around the yard with a red cup in my hand. As I reached down with it, he seemed to relate, "Whatever. If you really want it, here you go," and he filled the cup. I went over to the patio table and set Cody's sample down and picked up the empty cup for Dingo.

Now, if you know blue heelers, you know they follow their owners everywhere. Dingo, who had watched the collection process with Cody, took off in the yard with a look of disdain. I cajoled him, "Here, Dingo! Come on, boy." He was having none of it. I felt sure he was thinking, "You've got to be kidding me. Not today!"

I tried again the next morning (yes, with a similar outfit), but Dingo already had my number and quickly declined any opportunity to share his liquids with the vet. I still chuckle at the looks this dog gave me. Needless to say, I returned to the vet on Monday with only one sample, apologizing for my quirky dog. The staff laughed and understood. (For future reference, I later learned that the vet's secret weapon is a soup ladle—go figure!)

What could this possibly have to do with leadership? In the workplace, you also have tasks that your manager asks you to do that sound impossible and may cause you to look ridiculous in the process. I've found the most compelling trait that helps us get through difficult times in the workplace is a healthy sense of humor. The ability to laugh at ourselves will often be that icebreaker that starts building connection and trust. In fact, we'd

> *The ability to laugh at ourselves will often be that icebreaker that starts building connection and trust.*

do well to take our cues from children. As a mom, I've learned that they have mastered the belly laugh and teach us to be silly and laugh more often. A genuine smile or funny story can have a similar effect in the workplace.

One day not long after I moved to Florida, as I was walking about half a mile from my car to the office, I stopped to check out one of my shoes since it felt as if the heel had broken. I noticed it wasn't broken, so I kept walking. I was walking kind of funny but held my head high as if I were "all that" (leader that I am). About an hour later, I stopped to say hello to my two team leads. I looked down and noticed I had on mismatched shoes—two different heights *and* colors! "Oh, for the love of Pete!" I exclaimed as they laughed to tears while I walked—er, hobbled—back to my desk, face bright red from embarrassment. I retrieved my purse and told my friends, "I'm headed to lunch early." Then I hobbled my way back to my car, shaking my head with a smile on my face, wondering how I didn't notice this faux pas earlier. Then I drove to the closest shoe store for new shoes since it was closer than home.

If your office is like mine, you can relate and know that the story spread quickly. The remainder of the week I heard such comments as, "Nice shoes," or, "At least they're the same color today." Even better, and a bit humbling, was my friend's reenactment for others of my hobbling wearing two different shoes.

In the midst of crazy requests and stressful meetings, that story has also provided the short respite needed to keep moving forward. That humbling story that lets us laugh at ourselves also tends to remind those we lead that we're all human. Just as the hobble down the hallway gave my team a good laugh—and the unexpected task of collecting a doggie urine sample challenged my pride—it also reminded me to keep a sense of humor in every situation. This will be important in the picking-up-poop process, which begins in the next chapter.

–2–

Inside-Out Pickup

Getting Valuable Information from Others

As I started over in a new city living in temporary housing without a yard, I found myself in a new season as a dog walker and discovered that the poop bag has much utility. Thankfully, the apartment complex often provided an area for dogs to run a bit and have some freedom to do their business. Even so, my two dogs had quite the transition, since they moved from a large, fenced backyard that they had all to themselves to this chain-link-fence-surrounded area that contained many other dogs to investigate. It was a transition for me too. The first rule of apartment living with dogs: no more shovels. I now have little bags that go over my hands as I pick up my dogs' little brown gifts. While the grocery store bag may work, as most of us have experienced, the smaller bags can help with what I call the inside-out pickup.

To perform the inside-out pickup, you take the bag off the roll and (after you finally figure out which end will actually open) place the outside of the bag over your hand, then retrieve the poop from the grass, dirt, cement, or other surface. At this point, you have your treasure in the palm of your hand and can pull the edges of the bag over the top of your hand to have the bag ready for the big tie-off. (We'll talk about that next.) If not performed properly, it can get a bit messy (also a discussion for a later chapter). The inside-out pickup becomes tricky when you're out with two dogs on two leashes, since you only have two hands, after all. I highly recommend holding the leashes with the non-pickup hand to maintain a steady hand on the way up (preventing an unintended toss of the pickup before the flip of the bag's edges). My pooches eventually learned to wait for me to complete the pickup before moving forward to the next adventure.

You'll need to pick up the information dumps one "bag" at a time to really process the nuggets of knowledge that your predecessor provides.

Consider how this inside-out pickup might relate to the project at work you're picking up from your predecessor—the project you took on with cost, schedule, technical, and often people challenges that will give you a chance to grow your strengths over the next year or two. You'll need to pick up the information dumps one "bag" at a time to really process the nuggets of knowledge that your predecessor provides. The detail and value of the information you receive may depend on the timing of the transition and the attitude of the one handing off the project. Watch for clues that the "dog on the leash" is about to pull you in a different direction before you've completed this pickup. In most cases, you'll only get a few weeks with this individual to find out his or her approach to the project. I have found that taking lots of notes in your own format, especially about who knows what and who's who in the zoo, can be a more valuable pickup than some of the detailed information your predecessor might provide. Also, I try to take the time to understand my predecessor's organization, location, and strategies for storing data so I can still find key information long after he or she has left.

Regardless of how much information you pick up, if you go into this transition with an open mind and a willingness to form your own opinions, the clean slate you bring to the project might be just what folks need to be more successful. For example, on one project my predecessor had quite a bit of history with folks on the team. While I wanted to gain some of his insight concerning individual strengths and weaknesses, I also brought my own leadership style to the team and offered every team member an opportunity to start over with a clean slate. I recall mentioning at the first team meeting, "If you have any bad habits, now would be a good time to create some new, better habits." As a leader, you need to build trust with the individuals on the team on your terms, with your own perspective. Most people respond differently depending on the leadership style, so try to go in with an open mind every time.

As we'll see in later chapters, not everything you've picked up will help down the road. But if you've executed the inside-out pickup correctly, you'll have only a bag in your hand and not a mess on you. That leads us to the next topic: the tie-off.

–3–

The Tie-Off

Moving Forward

The tie-off of these little bags determines the quality of the rest of the walk. The goal is to make a quick knot without getting poop all over your hand. Similar to tying a knot at the end of a balloon, what normally does the trick is making a little twist and then a small loop around your index finger and then pulling the end back through the loop. With two dogs, I often had to carry a few filled bags for the rest of the walk, so the knots with clean tops made the bags easier (and less messy) to carry while holding a leash or two.

Now, this doesn't seem that difficult until one of the dogs starts pulling on the leash or you get an especially large load and have a smaller bag to tie off. New dog owners will agree that at the beginning the tie-off can be the more difficult part of the dog poop challenge. As I've seen with children inexperienced in tying balloons, tying the knot can be frustrating, even to the most coordinated—especially those with large fingers who have to deal with getting the end through the smaller loop.

In the workplace, the tie-off in a transition can also become one of the more frustrating tasks that a leader will face because it requires two leaders to focus on the exit of the former leader while trying to spin up the new leader. Similar to the military, where I was a commissioned officer, the corporate world tends to ask more of you every year—and suggests you take new positions or new challenges within your position every eighteen months to three years. While the military does a change-of-command ceremony to ensure everyone knows who has the command of the troops, in the corporate environment you are often expected to train your successor before you can move on. In the best-case scenario, you've been building your successor along the way and get to hand off the tasks to him or her fairly seamlessly. Other times, you need to make a change quickly. Quite a few workplace scenarios can drive a short transition timeline and limit conversations with the predecessor. In that instance, you will need to rely on your data mining and active listening skills as well as other members of your team to get up to speed in your new role.

Transferring to a new position within a company presents a

> *I've found that a transition schedule that covers three to six weeks can often give the right balance during the transition.*

unique challenge in negotiations. In this case, the tie-off can normally benefit from some planning and communication. I've found that a transition schedule that covers three to six weeks can often give the right balance during the transition. With a progressive allocation of time across projects (gradually transitioning to your new role), you should be able to give both projects enough attention to pick up your new duties while giving tasks away. The multi-week transition, which spans multiple regular business cycles, may be needed if you have financial tasks that require your successor to shadow you to learn. For example, you show the new person the task you've mastered while he or she shadows you, and then you turn the tables and let your successor perform the task while you provide support if needed.

In the past, I have used a model that allows for gradual assumption of new duties and a similar gradual handoff of the current role. Using the model in a practical example below, Sam is leaving Project X and going to Project Y with a three-week transition to Heidi, who is leaving Project Z and coming to Project X.

	Week 1	Week 2	Week 3	Week 4
Sam's time on his "old" Project, X	75%	50%	25%	Tied Off
Heidi's time on her "new" Project, X	25%	50%	75%	100%
Sam's time on his "new" Project, Y	25%	50%	75%	100%
Heidi's time on her "old" Project, Z	75%	50%	25%	Tied Off

This model can expand easily, if needed, to cover key milestones. To continue with the example, if Sam and Heidi document the plan, both of them will find it much easier to agree that the transition has completed. When Sam has shown all the tasks completed and has buy-in from Heidi, he should be able to walk away with a win-win outcome.

A couple of times I have taken the lead of the team I'm already on, and my predecessor remained on the team. This situation requires extra care and attention to help the team move forward while maintaining the relationship with your predecessor and the rest of the team. While every situation is unique, if you can establish and communicate boundaries and agree that your predecessor retains key tasks where he or she had expertise, you will normally overcome the initial awkward moments.

Regardless of your situation, remember the goal with the tie-off: you want to have a smooth transition that allows your predecessor to move on and enjoy his or her new role as you also move forward into your new role as the lead.

–4–

Throw It Away

Processing Feedback

Depending on where you live, where to throw away the dog poop can become quite the point of contention. In my youth, we just put it in the compost pile and let it fertilize the dead leaves. If you live in the city or a gated community, your neighbors get much more excited about where to throw away the poop. Clearly, if there's a poop bucket nearby, that's your best option.

If you're cleaning up the poop inside the house, a shortcut might be to pick up the poop with toilet paper and flush it, but I digress. The larger the bag, the tougher the choice. My quick consult with Google confirms that the debate continues.[2]

In leadership, whether it's in the workplace, your home office, or any other area of life where you lead, from time to time you have a need to "throw it away." Many nuggets and stories come to mind. If recently you have moved due to a new job, had to clear out someone else's house due to a death in the family, or moved your kids to college, you may find yourself faced with difficult throwaway situations. (The list can be overwhelming). A change of scenery can often motivate us to clear out the mess and make room for something new. In a very practical sense, I found that you have to make some phone calls to find the right place to throw away those forgotten garage items that have become hazardous. Even tougher can be figuring out what to do with old electronics or dead trampolines. While it isn't difficult to decide to dispose of poop, I sometimes have a tough time going through the other waste I may have collected. But just like dog poop, it gets accomplished one pickup, one bag at a time.

In the workplace, we get feedback—sometimes too much, sometimes very little. Either way, negative feedback can have a lasting impact and can be the toughest to throw away. Yes, you even need to eventually get rid of positive feedback because it can fill you up and not help you. So enjoy the positive feedback of the day, but don't hold onto it; stay humble.

I had a mentor who gave me very valuable feedback. We used to have a block for positive feedback—what we're doing well, strengths to continue honing. We also had a block for negative feedback—weaknesses or blind spots we needed to work on. That mentor (and manager) had the same statement for me in both blocks: "You're a very strong communicator." He went on to point out that I needed to keep working on what we call "soft skills" these days. I needed to find the balance of when to come on strong and when to give someone else the best story of the day and just listen. I'm still working on this one, and I suspect it will be something that continues to challenge me.

In contrast, a few years ago, I had a different manager tell me that I no longer had much potential. That negative message stuck with me for a long time—this is the type of feedback we want to throw away quickly! In his book *Leadershift*, John C. Maxwell points out that

> Maybe as leaders we need to recognize the value of "mental floss." Dentists encourage us to use dental floss daily to promote the health of our teeth; we need to use mental floss to get rid of old thinking and promote the health of our leadership. . . .
>
> For years I had a sign in my office that said, "Yesterday Ended Last Night." I put it there to remind me that all the good I did yesterday won't guarantee a good day for me today, nor will all the bad that happened yesterday mean that today has to be bad. Today stands on its own. If I want a great today, I need to do what's necessary now. I can and should be grateful for yesterday, but I have to focus on today.[3]

As I processed the messages in his book and began to apply his insights, I took away a key nugget. We shouldn't let our emotions, both good and bad, consume us, but rather we should process them for a day, then throw them out and start with a fresh perspective the next day. On the great days, take the time to celebrate with others; then let go of those emotions. On the tough days, choose which hill to climb, which battles to fight, which messages to apply, and then let those emotions go.

Navigating the naysayers and manipulators can be one of the toughest things to do in your life. Whether you call him or her a friend or a colleague, when someone builds your trust and then rips off one's mask to reveal one's true motivations, it can leave you reeling. Unfortunately, I have had to navigate a few difficult and undermining situations—mostly in the workplace. When the angst and rejection, rumor mills or deception starts, guard your heart and seek wise council from a trusted mentor or friend who knows you well. Your own actions and words can often influence the situation in ways you might not expect.

> *We shouldn't let our emotions, both good and bad, consume us, but rather we should process them for a day, then throw them out and start with a fresh perspective the next day.*

I'm not suggesting we throw away authentic friendships; however, setting boundaries will go a long way in keeping your emotions on level ground. So process your emotions, have the difficult and honest conversations—either with yourself or with others—to resolve negative feedback, and then throw it away and let it go.

What Happens When the Bag Breaks?

Embrace a New Perspective

Yep, we're there. On more than one occasion (albeit limited to a handful of times), I prepared for the inside-out pickup, and as I reached down and closed my hand around the pile, I felt something warm and slimy. "Yuck!" (OK, depending on how my day was going, one may have heard a few other words.) The dogs would just look at me with that face that says, "What's the big deal?" I tried to minimize the leakage by getting another bag, but the damage was done. So I relied on my early camping and army experience and worked with what I had available. I contained the mess with another bag and then found grass, a leaf, an active sprinkler—anything, really—to get as much as possible off my hands.

As part of my move to Florida, I spent about forty-five days in a hotel with Dingo and Cody. We took the four flights of stairs five or six times a day and into the night, rain or shine. After more than one broken bag, I started carrying hand sanitizer with me! And I solved the breaking bags somewhat when I started buying my own bags. Then I finally had a house again and the dogs were thrilled to have a yard to run around in.

In most situations, the "broken bag" is just a bump in the road that makes the day a little more humbling. I can relate it to those conversations that start with, "We need to talk." Maybe it's a performance feedback session that breaks the news that you're not getting the raise you expected. Maybe it's the loved one walking away. Maybe it's the last-straw comment that sends you to your favorite stress-relieving routine (in my case, likely Schlotzsky's or Chick-fil-A). Either way, the bag breaks, and you hold it in as long as you can, then walk away for a bit to get perspective.

On the other hand, what if the bag breaks but the poop misses you? What if the conversation hits the mark and confirms you nailed it and landed the promotion? Just like that new backyard or dog park that sparks pure joy in our pups, a well-timed encouraging word can last so much longer if we let it sink in. For years I've found it difficult to smile and say thank you when someone gives me positive feedback. As a leader, I've learned a new approach and look for opportunities to celebrate successes.

In corporate America, others often want you to pick a path—either technical or management. As you may guess, I've had assignments in both for most of my career. In one of my first civilian positions, I was told, "You've got really great leadership skills, but we're not so sure about your technical skills." Since I was in my late twenties working for a very technical company, I took my next assignment to advance and build my technical skills. Fast-forward a few years, and—yep, you guessed it—now I received the feedback "She's great technically, but we're not sure about her leadership skills." I've learned to embrace my unique skill set and take positions that need both technical depth and project management.

When the bag breaks and you hit that bump in the road, it may challenge your patience and creativity for a little while; however, it will always give you an opportunity to embrace a new perspective.

When the bag breaks and you hit that bump in the road, it may challenge your patience and creativity for a little while; however, it will always leave you with a choice on how to react and give you an opportunity to embrace a new perspective.

–6–

Get a Light

Invite New Insights to the Situation

I f you've ever walked your dogs after the sun went down or before it came up, you know how quickly you can lose sight of the poop while you get the bag. A few times I had the bags in one pocket and my phone in another. The dogs began pulling on their leashes, ready to continue their search for frogs in the dark. I reached into the pocket for the bag, got ready to pick up, and then lost the poop in the grass. Yes, I pulled out my phone and turned on the flashlight. From afar, I'm sure it looked pretty funny seeing a grown woman searching in the grass with a cell phone flashlight in one hand and a poop bag at the ready in the other. Combine that with a broken bag, and an onlooker might see some entertaining dancing in the dark.

Practically speaking, bringing light to a leadership situation can solve many issues. For example, I have stared at a section of code for hours and had a coworker look at it and see the problem right away. In the corporate world, we use peer reviews to formally inspect a work product such as a document or a portion of software code. I fully embrace that a peer review will always help any product. From a leadership perspective, I learned quickly that a second set of eyes can point out the words that will offend, fill in the blanks for clarity, and often find that missing comma or misspelled word.

If you're in the middle of writing one of those potentially career-limiting emails, a peer review becomes essential. If you don't have a trusted friend or lead nearby, let it sit overnight, and give it another look before hitting "Send." You will almost always find a way to say it better with a second look. You may decide that the issue should be discussed in a face-to-face conversation instead or that the email should just get deleted.

Perhaps that peer review turns into a tense meeting. Sometimes I use a common funny story to lighten up a meeting. Other times, I just seize the opportunity to find the humor in a situation. One afternoon I needed to support a weekly telecon from home. I remained on mute until it was my turn to brief my chart. I started to speak, took a quick pause, and said, "Excuse me." Immediately after that, Cody, who was sitting beside my chair, decided to deliver one of the loudest dog belches I'd ever heard. Of course, as I tried to continue, I told them that was the dog and started to giggle. One of the others said, "Sure it was," and joined me in laughter. I had to hit the mute button. When I could stop laughing with tears in my eyes, I returned to the call and excused the dog, again, and attempted to continue the meeting. One of my colleagues told me later that no one on the call believed it was the dog, and they continued to laugh on mute. We have used that story often to lighten the tone of a meeting.

When leading from the middle, we need to be that light. We need to bring the energy and fresh perspective to keep the team moving forward. We also need to invite others to bring their light into our blind spots. When we allow others to collaborate and join the conversation, we open the door for them to grow as well. If you include the stakeholders in the plan before you

> *When leading from the middle, we need to be that light. We need to bring the energy and fresh perspective to keep the team moving forward.*

move forward, you will get much-needed feedback, a better product, and buy-in from all involved. For instance, we had a very tight schedule with many stakeholders and incredible visibility. We decided to embrace their perspectives and set up a collaboration session to walk through the schedule. We went line by line and looked at every task for dependencies, considering whether that task needed another task to complete before it started (e.g., delayed hardware must be received before software can be installed on the hardware). We also discussed every assumption in detail (e.g., duration and resources required to install the hardware and software based on prior experience). We added a facilitator to assist with the potentially contentious conversations. We also looked at the schedule from a couple of different perspectives. The first pass went top-down, reviewing every task, duration, and dependency. Then, the next day, we looked again from the end working backward and revisited the dependencies and assumptions. The bottom-up pass (no pun intended) caught some key dependencies we had missed the day before. Also, as we executed the plan, with the light shed on the project from the beginning, the stakeholders had better insight into the complexities and challenges ahead. The prior coordination and collaboration continued to illuminate key off-ramps (i.e., considering alternate hardware suppliers) and guide contingency decisions as we met the critical milestones.

Collaboration is a valuable tool we can use to shed light on a difficult problem and help inform our decisions.

–7–

Scoop It Up

Own Your Choices

I f you have a yard and dogs, you likely have a pooper-scooper. Pooper-scoopers come in many sizes and differ in capability. In my opinion, they're a must-have in a yard with two or more dogs. I like the rake option on the smaller scooper to get the most coverage. The ones that take the bag as an insert can make the throwaway process a little easier. However, sometimes you encounter a different kind of scooping situation.

One day not long after I moved from the hotel into the house, I took Cody and Dingo to the neighborhood dog park. A black Lab puppy about six months old was having a blast running around. His ears flopped as he ran. His tongue flapped to the side of his mouth. Cody went to one end of the park and took care of business. I walked over to the bag stand to get a bag. While I was prepping the bag, that young Lab came running at full speed and stopped right in front of Cody's poop. He smelled it, as dogs do, and then he slurped it right up! That's one way to scoop it up! Gagging yet? I certainly did.

The slurping session reminds me of when I have been the younger energetic leader who naively volunteered to take over a project in hopes of getting that treasured visibility. However, my decision to dive in without fully understanding the issues or the culture quickly backfired. In a more recent case, it occurred when I interviewed for a new position out of town and had limited insight into the issues that surrounded the project that I found myself leading.

Even when moving internally, you should take the time to understand and ask questions about the position. After you think you have a solid understanding of the position, sit down and do more homework. I highly recommend some time with a pad of paper and a pen. I write the pros on one side and cons on the other. Then I proceed to fill in both columns for leaving and staying. After I've written it all down, I set it aside and let it brew overnight. When we sleep on any major decision, we get additional clarity with a fresh set of eyes. Pick up the list and take another look. If you still have questions or reservations about the decision, seek wise counsel. If, after talking with a trusted mentor or friend about it, you still don't have peace and excitement about the decision, perhaps it's time to reconsider your answer. However, sometimes the situation may call for you to scoop up the opportunity and exercise some creativity.

For example, one morning as I went downstairs to get more coffee after my shower, I noticed something in the pool. I threw some shoes on and ventured out to the pool deck with wet hair. In hindsight I really should've gone up and changed out of my robe before investigating further. But then you wouldn't enjoy the story as much. Anyway, you guessed it; I looked in the shallow end and found a large mound that appeared to have fallen in the pool, still in solid form. I walked over and picked up the skimmer net with a six-foot pole on the end. I dipped the skimmer net into the water, and with the first scoop, I found that the solid had turned to mush! I scooped with the skimmer and came up with soupy poop, which I proceeded to flick through the patio screen to the grass... or that was my plan, anyway. After about five to ten scoops with the skimmer, I had most of it out of the pool and had managed to avoid getting any poop on me. I went to the screened-in patio to get chemicals (yes, still in my robe and boat shoes, wet hair now almost dry) and noticed that any of my neighbors could've been watching. Mortified, I waved at a car as it rolled by, but I never heard a neighbor mention it. Then I put a triple shock of chemicals in the pool and took another shower. It now qualifies as a good watercooler story. I have learned to use the vacuum instead of the "soupy scoop" and backwash the filter afterward.

Both of these "scoop" situations remind me of a trip to an ice cream parlor. As soon as I walked through the door, the chilly air cooled my skin as I pondered my choices. One scoop or two? What flavor? And then I found the list of toppings—so many choices! If I felt adventurous like that young puppy, I might choose a two-scoop sugar cone with the new "special" flavors of the day, which look good in the freezer. On other days, I might choose my favorite in the cup, either out of habit as the safe choice, or just because I know what I want. I recall one time when my siblings and I went for ice cream with my grandmother. I was seven or eight years old and knew that I wanted the green mint chocolate chip. I found it behind the glass, pointed to my choice, and selected the sugar cone as usual. I waited my turn, and as I stepped outside, I took that first cold taste. I had selected the pistachio instead! With the long line behind us, I had to own my choice and try something new. I also learned that I still prefer a scoop of mint chocolate chip over pistachio.

In leading others and in life, we will experience disappointments and setbacks. Regardless of the situation, we must accept responsibility for our choices. After my parents' divorce, I grew up with my father. He wasn't a big fan of the blame game. He used to tell me that I was the only one who could choose how I felt or reacted to what happened. When I became upset, or angry at what someone else said or did, I had to own my reaction. By the time I was a teenager, I started taking his advice to heart.

I became quite independent and learned to own my choices. No longer did I blame my parents for what had happened to me or how well I did in school. I owned my decisions.

How you choose at an important crossroads can change the trajectory of your career or even your life. Whatever you choose, only you can take responsibility for your choices and their consequences. Anyone who has stood in a court of law or dealt with the legal system understands this concept. In some cases, others may stifle, block, or even seemingly remove your choices. The longer this continues to happen, the harder it becomes to resist and change. For example, burnout doesn't happen all at once. It happens slowly, one choice at a time. Even not having a voice is making a choice or allowing someone else to do it for you. In any situation, we should make the best possible choice with the information we have at the time.

If we're honest, each of us can point to key choices that affected our lives. And in hindsight we discover both the positive and negative effects of our decisions. I'd like to share a few life-changing choices I've made that have shaped my perspective. When conversations go down the path of regrets—you know the ones, the "coulda, woulda, shoulda" chats—I often share this story. In high school, I had been a competitive swimmer from age seven who had seen some real success. My freshman year the coach set high expectations, and though I swam my lifetime best by four seconds, I still missed the state competition by one-tenth of a second. I felt that I had failed because I didn't make it to the state competition. While it pushed me to try harder, it also clouded my pros and cons list for years with doubt and "if only". I continued to swim competitively for the remaining three years of high school and continued to just miss the next level of competition.

As a freshman in college, a totally different challenge was set before me: earn an NMMI slot to Airborne school. Of course, my competitive side kicked in full force when a few other women also said yes during that first week of sign-ups. Not long after my other female peers walked away, it became a "prove it" milestone for me. I should clarify: earning this slot meant really running with the men and keeping up with them during the three-mile runs in boots and when doing pushups, sit-ups, and any other exercises our cadre could come up with. While the physical demands were grueling in springtime in the desert, the mental toughness as the only female took self-doubt to a whole new level. There were no handouts for being female. To get into jump school, I had to pass the more difficult standards of the men. The message from the military school and cadre: if you fail and wash out, don't bother to come back to school in the fall. As a scholarship cadet, I was putting it all on the line, and an injury or washout would crush my goals to see active duty as a commissioned officer in the US Army.

I recall standing in formation with a company of Navy SEALs in mid-July at Fort Benning, Georgia. After six months of preparation, I was right back in the mental test of a lifetime. For the next two weeks, we'd have a week of ground training, learning how to land. That was followed by a week of tower training, learning how to jump out of the plane (one thousand one, one thousand two, one thousand three, one thousand four, one thousand five, one thousand six, and the static line pulls your parachute open). The third week was the coveted jump week. By the fifth jump, the mental toughness said, "Even if I crash and burn, I still get my wings." I enjoy telling that story because at nineteen years old, I overcame every "coulda, woulda, shoulda" with a "yep, I did that (and lived to tell the story)!" I earned my jump wings in August 1984. For the next few decades, that milestone encouraged me and gave me the ability to dig deep in the face of tough days and tough choices. While this saying has become a bit cliché, it is of course true: we will certainly fail at 100 percent of the things we refuse to try. From a leadership perspective, those wings provided an instant measure of respect while in uniform as well as in industry. I've had more than one person learn this about me and change their perspective and look again at the potential in front of them.

Like most people, I've made some unpopular and tough choices. A few years after jump school, I was an officer who had graduated with Distinguished Military Graduate honors and had earned the highest performance ratings the year before during my first full active-duty assignment in Germany. I chose my spouse and gave up my military career

We will certainly fail at 100 percent of the things we refuse to try.

as a commissioned officer and became an enlisted wife. I had to start over again in the civilian world. Four months later, I was a pregnant newlywed in a foreign country and totally dependent on my husband and humbled. At the time, giving up my military career felt like a huge failure. However, this story and the others showed me that we may not see the full impact of our choices until much later in life. Though my choice with the military may have been unpopular, it kept me from a war, and our daughter's health kept my husband from that war as well in late 1990. Then, I spent the next three years rebuilding my career using my fallback plan with my computer science degree. After the military moved us to Colorado, I managed to land on my feet as a leader supporting the

DOD. I can credit much of my leadership training to the training I received in my years in the military.

When faced with tough choices or tough changes in life, we need to understand the landscape and may need to adjust our approach, which you will learn more about in the next chapter.

—8—

Understand the Landscape

Adjust Your Approach to Fit the Team

When we lived in Colorado, I took the pooches on long walks, mostly on the trails. Colorado Springs has a large park on the side of a mountain ridge right in the middle of town called Palmer Park. About a month after we adopted Cody, I decided to take Dingo and Cody for a walk on a trail through the rocks and ridges in Palmer Park. They were listening to my voice and doing so well on the trail that I decided to let them off the leash while we were up in the rocky area. Both stayed close, and all was well...until they heard something down the hill in the woods off the trail. Off they went at full speed into the brush. Of course, I started calling them right away. Dingo came right back after about five minutes. Cody, however, must have been having too much fun running free and chasing critters in the woods. I called and called, "Coooody! Cooooody!" as I continued to walk the trail. Dingo helped every so often by barking. I started thinking, "We've only had this dog a month, and I've already lost him." I even enlisted a few others on the trail to be on the lookout for him. After about thirty minutes of calling, Cody finally came running up the trail. I was so relieved to see him again that I couldn't even get mad. Despite this, I returned with the dogs often to Palmer Park and other longer trails, but I never had that problem again, since with practice they had become used to hearing my voice and staying near my side.

Another time, they managed to get through a few loose boards in the fence. The neighbors commented that it looked as if they were walking themselves as they trotted down the sidewalk. This happened a couple of different times before we could get the fence fixed. Both times, they quickly found themselves miles away from home and loving the run.

As I mentioned, with the move from Colorado to Florida, Dingo and Cody experienced hotel living and a long road trip for the first time. We left quite late that first evening and only managed to drive about three hours before it was time to pull over and stay at a hotel for the night. Neither dog had ever been in a hotel, and now we had them on an elevator headed to the third floor. While we had no incidents in the hotel, both dogs and humans spent the next four days adapting to long drives with short walks.

At the end of the long drive, they had to adapt to living in a one-bedroom apartment and walks to the midsize dog run. We finally managed the routine of three or four walks per day. Most of the time, they would wait, very excited, at the double gate until I let them off the leash in the dog run. The dog run provided bags for the pickups and a receptacle for waste. Dingo and Cody had to adjust and make new friends in a confined space. We spent sixty days in that apartment while I searched for a house with a fenced-in backyard.

Before I found the house, my lease was up at the apartment, and I found myself in a bit of a homeless situation, living in a hotel for forty-five days with the dogs. The landscape, routine, and walks changed again. Our mornings started early with a quick trip down the stairs from the fourth floor to prevent any mishaps before we could get outside. Most of the time, we walked around the hotel across an empty lot and by the back hedges. Though the hotel provided a bag station on one side, I also carried extras in my pocket. When I had more time, in the evenings, we took longer walks on a trail that went around the lake behind the hotel. Once in a while, we saw snakes, among other critters (but that's the topic of another chapter).

Finally, four months after starting our journey from Colorado to Florida, we had a house with a pool and a fenced backyard. Then the walks became a little longer and less frequent, since the dogs could roam freely in their yard. Unlike at our previous house, we began to keep our eyes open for alligators and angry birds.

The point is, with each change of the landscape, I had a different pickup strategy and had to adapt my approach.

Leading from the middle has many of the same challenges. Every team, every assignment presents a new opportunity to find a new approach and make adjustments while leading the team. Whether you're taking over a new team or assuming the lead role on your current team, you have to understand your level of influence to determine your approach. If you're a new leader on a team, you won't have much influence.

> *Every team, every assignment presents a new opportunity to find a new approach and make adjustments while leading the team.*

Many people have defined *leadership* as influence. I've also heard (and experienced) that when you lose your influence, it's time to move on. On my journey, I have experienced both sides of influence. It can take a while to earn influence; however, some will grant their trust and acceptance readily. But if you ever lose or break that trust, conversations can quickly turn into tense situations and awkward silence. It reminds me a lot of quicksand. The more you try to solve the problem and explain yourself, the tougher it gets.

So how do we gain influence?

When I've had the most influence and when I've enjoyed the teams the most, I've taken the time to get to know those on my team. Your approach will be as unique as you are. You may have to—no, you *will* have to—adjust your approach, depending on the person. Most of all, I urge you to start with the simple stuff. Learn their names. Share something about yourself to break the ice. Find some common ground. Look them in the eyes and listen. Early in my time as a software lead, I lost touch with this important point and spent more time on the project details than on the people. When I didn't give as much time to the person and maintaining our relationship, the conversations and productivity suffered. I had one manager who was very good at that initial connection with people and became very intentional by sending us all a questionnaire asking about personal details. Then he used that to learn our birthdays and other special days. Hopefully you know at least one person on the team as you begin your transition as the leader. Once, I took on the lead role for a team that had recently combined a couple of teams and had about one-third of the team at another location in a different time zone. After a couple of weeks of learning their names, I had to get creative to figure out how to get this team to find some common ground. My first team meeting as the leader fell on my birthday. I found an icebreaker question that could work well on the phone. In a telecon with approximately thirty-five engineers in the conference room with me and another twenty engineers on the phone, I gave each of them the opportunity to introduce themselves and share their current position, what they worked on, and their favorite ice cream or frozen treat. I took detailed notes, then presented them with metrics on their ice cream choices at the next meeting. (In case you're wondering, vanilla won.) However, I had a few responses that I still recall. One person answered, "I'm more of an ice cream buffet guy—just love them all." Another replied, "Red bean ice cream." I replied, "Really? I didn't even know that was a flavor." I became very good friends with both of them. The team then decided it was their thing. Every person who joined the team while I was the lead had to provide his or her favorite ice cream flavor. I enjoyed incredible influence with this team.

Whatever your personal style, to gain influence, you must be authentic. The better you know someone, the quicker you can recognize when the person is distracted, needs to go get the kids, or is having a rough day. I've found that a little encouragement goes a long way and makes you a more effective leader. And the next time you have a peak season for productivity, your team members will say yes, especially if you're working right beside them. They will say yes because you've already invested the time in them. As a software lead, I find myself leading very intelligent people who will rarely respond favorably to "because I said so" leadership.

Conversely, when burnout after long days filled with frustration and rants sneaks in, our influence starts to erode and will eventually dry up. For example, early in my career, we were changing—overhauling, really—our delivery process to streamline it. I was leading a team of twelve software developers, and we'd just completed a release that managed to get all our fixes in on time. We'd finally felt as if we operated like a well-oiled machine. I recall a bit of grumbling on my part about the new process. Then one day things changed. My manager asked to speak with me and said, "Shut the door, please." This conversation made a lasting impact on my leadership style and view of influence. She said, "I need you to get on board with this new process. Your endorsement will help it succeed. But your grumbling about it will ensure a rocky start and certain failure."

Then she assigned a few of the new-process writing tasks to

me, so I had to own them. I took a few things from that experience. I stopped complaining and went into the new process tasks with an open mind. (I may have had additional motivation since it was now part of my next performance evaluation.) The other nugget I picked up: the loudest and most frequent complainer may be your best ally when you're trying to shift or change the culture.

A few years later, I had a couple of different situations where I was the leader and someone on my team made many "suggestions." Learning from my previous manager, I flipped it on him and gave him the task with full responsibility and ownership. I found the grumbling stopped and the ownership became empowering and motivating. While I still had to provide some boundaries and guidance on the overall vision, I gave the whole task to him, which allowed him to bring unique insights and give voice to his passion.

When you find yourself leading a team, work to improve your influence and adjust your approach to build connections with your team members and ultimately ensure the success of the project.

–9–

Get a Bigger Bag

Embrace a Bigger Vision

Of course, the size of the bag you'll need really depends on the size of the dog or dogs, the surrounding landscape, and how long it's been since you spent any time picking up poop. If I haven't picked up poop in the yard in a while, I start with the large leaf bag. Friends with very large dogs mention that even for walks, they need to use the grocery-size plastic bags for the pickup. I would definitely recommend inspecting the bag for little holes before using the crumbled grocery bags from the recycle bag of bags.

Let's say you've found yourself in a situation where you have more poop than bag. You've already made the decision, or you were asked to come in and "fix it." Depending on the situation, "fix it" often means a project needs a kick-start, it's fallen behind, or maybe it just needs a different leadership style to take it over the finish line. I've walked through each of these scenarios. In every "fix it" assignment, I've had to look for creative ways to motivate the team. I've had to get a "bigger bag," a bigger vision, and then find a unique way to articulate it to the team.

Early in my career, I could see the finish line and would jump in and share my thoughts, sometimes without waiting for others to finish. I would be excited for the idea and unable to wait to share my thoughts. The colleague I interrupted would shut it down quickly, not seeing the bigger picture I could see unfolding. After a very good friend watched this happen for a few months, he shared something wise that still gets me to pause and start again. He said, "You see the vision so quickly, and the rest of us are still back at the first step and don't see where you're taking us. When you take the time to walk it through in smaller steps, the whole team catches the vision with you." I've really tried to embrace his advice over the last twenty years and often share it with others. I still get ideas I want to share right away, but I've found some alternatives to interrupting. Because I don't want to forget those fleeting thoughts (in case there's a good idea there), I make sure I keep a pencil and paper handy in most meetings. When I get those thoughts, I tend to go ahead and write them down with a "me" next to them or maybe "note to self" in the margin. Then, when the opportunity presents itself, I can share the idea in a more organized way.

Another time I needed to get a bigger bag, or vision, was when we had a large deadline looming that would require a retest of the full system, which still had too many issues. As one of my coworkers and I walked down the hall, he asked, "What if we don't make it?" I replied, "What if we do? What if we pull it off?" That very moment, he started thinking about what it would take to accomplish our goal instead of about all the ways we couldn't do it. As leaders, we carry the hope and belief that we can meet the goals, even surpass them—and we have the ability to influence others, passing along that hope and belief to them. On days when that influence dries up, or we no longer believe we can accomplish something, we must dig deep to see the bigger picture and revive that hope again.

> *As leaders, we carry the hope and belief that we can meet the goals, even surpass them—and we have the ability to influence others, passing along that hope and belief to them.*

–10–

Now You've Stepped in It

Dealing with Unexpected Messy Situations

S ometimes you wake up to big messy poops first thing in the morning. You know the ones—they may start where you step off the stairs and extend all the way to the door. Whether slimy and almost dried or just plain slimy, it will take a while to clean up. With my older pooches, I found it might be a sign to get them to the vet. With a new puppy in the house, though, it can be expected (deep sigh) until training is complete. I tend to be the first one awake at my house, so normally that means I walk down the stairs in the dark while my eyes adjust to the day. One morning, I could feel the squish as I stepped off that bottom step. Ew! I may have uttered a few choice exclamations that should

47

never be repeated. Needless to say, that's not my favorite way to fully wake up—and before coffee! Now, the whole routine veers off track, as you must first get all poop remnants off your feet or house shoes, then off the rug, the tile, anywhere you may have tracked it. All the while, the pooch who left you a package waits not so patiently to go outside again.

One time Cody snuck up behind me in the kitchen and just started pooping. However, in his stealthy follow mode, he caught me quite unaware. I took half a step back and started sliding across the tile, my foam shoes slipping right across that poop. I stood there in a half split, not sure whether to laugh or cry. Cody just kept moving across the room, making a bigger mess. The cleanup took some time—the shoes, the tile, the carpet. Yuck! When my grown daughter walked into the kitchen after she heard my groan, she asked, "What happened?" She walked a little closer around the island in the kitchen and said, "Oh no." I'd found myself sort of stuck and surrounded by poop. One of my shoes wouldn't escape the muck with my foot, so I hopped out of it and tiptoed around the mess while requesting some help in the form of a roll of paper towels and disinfecting wipes. Between the gagging came giggles, then another deep sigh.

In many situations in life, both in the workplace and in other roles where you must take the lead, you might feel as if you've "stepped in it." Many related stories come to my mind. For example, as I navigated a divorce, I was reminded of a season of poop pickup at every turn—from the credit cards, to the bank accounts, to the kids, to the routines. Every day seems to bring a new challenge. My divorce came in the middle of a very dark time in my life, on the tail of the deaths of my parents as well as my grandmother, who spent much of her life as my "mother" as well. We also lost two dogs during those three years. Loss, guilt, and regret took me into a deep pit. Everyone looks for an escape from the pain. I chose to cope with fiction novels and good friends. On a calm afternoon in Colorado when I called in desperation, one friend gave me a great checklist to help me know if I could get through another day or needed to seek further counseling. I now call this a survival mode checklist of questions: 1) Are the kids getting fed and going to school? 2) Are the dogs getting fed? 3) Are you eating? 4) Are you sleeping? 5) Are you getting out of bed, showering, and going to work?

If you can answer yes to all of these, you're surviving. Some days that might be as good as it gets. But one day at a time, you start doing better than surviving and start thriving.

In the workplace, we often call these assignments where you've stepped in it the red programs. They almost feel like quicksand— every meeting turns up another issue that must be addressed. Cost and schedule pressures begin to extend the days and weeks ahead. Survival mode may set in quickly without a change in perspective. While I haven't gone through a bankruptcy, I can imagine that it might fall in this category as well. These situations become life changers.

So how do you deal with the mess? Like the elephant—one pickup, one mess at a time, knowing that at some point the scene will look different. When I have walked through some of my toughest transitions, I've found that words from a good friend have helped me immensely. Some days we go through the day in survival mode and just keep showing up and picking up.

As leaders, we really don't get to have bad days. These are the days and months, maybe even years, when you watch your words carefully lest they return in unwanted ways. On those tough days, in those tough seasons, I've found it really helps to have a trusted friend or mentor in your corner for support. Ask that friend to go for coffee, a meal out, whatever works, and talk about it. Perhaps take the dogs for a long walk and enjoy their pure delight in life. Stepping *out* of the situation and taking breaks such as these, along with leaning on support from trusted friends and mentors, will give you the energy and perspective to move forward out of survival mode and into thriving mode. Sometimes the best way to deal with a messy situation is to avoid it altogether.

> *On those tough days, in those tough seasons, I've found it really helps to have a trusted friend or mentor in your corner for support.*

–11–

No Way Am I Picking That Up!

Becoming Unoffendable

Have you ever walked into a room and smelled a mess before you saw it? Sometimes you step in it; other times you smell it and see where it landed and just, well, start gagging. Depending on what it landed on, that throw rug, towel, or favorite T-shirt may be destined for the trash can—and quickly. Even the pickup of the disgusting item will keep you gagging. In our house, whoever gags the least tends to get the vote for the cleanup duties (and that's normally me). One night I returned from a business trip to my adult children apologizing for the missing kitchen rug. "Sorry, Mom. Dingo had a rough night. It was everywhere! That rug had to go." Sometimes in the yard, the slippery slope of poop on the shoe, filling every crevice, has the same challenge—after a quick rinse with the hose, the shoes find a new permanent home in the garage for yard work. Other times, I've found the dog had thrown up all over a blanket or towel in its crate. The blanket had a direct trip to a large plastic bag with the tie-off, and both the dog and crate were taken out to the backyard with a hose and soap.

On a few occasions I have been on a walk, and one of the dogs has had a bit of runny poop in the middle of a thunderstorm or on the trail. You know the type—a big pile that oozes more than normal and reminds you of picking up mushy brown goop. Even my best attempts have left more on the grass than in the bag. After debating the consequences of my choices, I admit that I have left those piles for nature to wash away.

If we're being honest, no one looks forward to picking up poop, whether it's actual dog poop or workplace "poop"—an uncomfortable situation, a difficult conversation, an accusation, a snide remark that leaves you doubting your worth. The fresher the hurt or conversation, the more it sticks and has the power to drive your future perspective. For example, once after I taught a class, I picked up the surveys and saw that someone wrote that I should dress more professionally to make a better impression. That one comment drove me to second-guess my wardrobe choices for the next fifteen years.

If the "poop" is cleaned up quickly, it loses its ability to cause more issues. If we allow it to remain a little while, it may scoop up quicker, but it will leave something behind, potentially something that someone else will step in and that will cause more trouble for others. If it remains long enough, it becomes part of the landscape and invisible. It gets down deep into the dirt, and as it breaks down, it leaves some good and some bad behind. Every situation has the potential to stick as an offense. However, how long it takes to recognize and deal with it determines whether it becomes the chip on our shoulder, blind spot, or trigger for more pain. Offenses should be

Offenses should be quickly thrown away.

quickly thrown away. Choosing the high road with a little extra grace and change in perspective reveals our character as leaders and can defuse a tense conversation or situation.

In addition, every situation has the potential for learning and growing. As leaders in the middle, we need to recognize that every conversation has the power to encourage others, to motivate them to become the best version of themselves. As a younger leader, I could be very assertive and competitive, an attribute often expected and welcome in most military settings. However, I have learned through experience that just about everywhere else does not welcome the assertive approach. While we sometimes need to let that side come out, it doesn't need to be our first response. When we focus only on getting the task done without an eye on the people, we could miss out on opportunities to give those encouraging words, to build the team.

One way to make the connection is to ask open-ended questions. For example, I asked my team members an icebreaker question to get a better understanding of what drove them. I asked, "If you were to win the lottery tomorrow—we're talking big money that would never require another day in the office—what would you be doing? What hobby, passion, or dream do you have that you'd pursue?" Among a group of software development leads, I found that I had an amateur photographer,

Everyone has a unique strength that is necessary to keep the team moving forward.

found that I had an amateur photographer, a sailing captain, and someone who wanted to rescue lions and tigers. On a different team, during a season of incredible pressure, I asked the team members to give their minds a break for a few minutes and then asked them, "If you had unlimited funds, where in the world—anywhere in the world—would you want to go?" Within about ten minutes, our team traveled the world to places I never would have considered. I connected with my team members on another level while encouraging them.

I learned early that everyone has something to offer. Everyone has a unique strength that is necessary to keep the team moving forward. As a leader, it helps to find those teammates who cover the gaps and your weaknesses. If you have a task you really don't enjoy and, frankly, struggle with, find someone on the team who enjoys it, and let the teammate pick up the task and own it. Your team member will likely surprise you. You may find that the task gets completed faster and better with that delegation and your team member feels confident in his or her role. However, sometimes it may make more sense to look outside your team or your organization to fill the gaps.

–12–

Pay Someone Else to Do It

Count the Cost

Sometimes we have a season in which we need extra help. Whether we have a large or small yard, a big or little job, we have opportunities to take a different approach. It takes humility to allow someone to come into the middle of your mess and clean it up. Pride often keeps me from asking others to help with something like picking up dog poop. However, I have experienced summers when I have had more money than time to spend out in the sun picking up poop. While I understand that pet owners need to plan for this extra chore when they decide to have a dog, sometimes life throws us curveballs and busy seasons—activities, vacations, physical limitations...the list can grow quickly—that keep us from being able to complete this task. A willing teenager or friend in a tough spot looking for odd jobs may finish the job more quickly than you and really appreciate the extra cash.

However, you need to consider all the costs before bringing in an expert. One summer we hired a small business to help with the weekly mowing. The company had one requirement: that the yard had no dog poop, and they did not offer to help with the pickup for an extra fee. Although we gained the time it took to mow a large lot, we had to rake up the dog poop more often than we might have had we kept the whole task for ourselves.

Once I even called in help for a human poop problem, which is probably my most disgusting poop story. One morning after my divorce, I went down to the basement and found the sewage gurgling back up the drain. I tried the plunger when the puddle was small. As you can imagine, that plan backfired—more sewage oozed in the small utility closet with the hot water heater and furnace. By the time I could call a plumber to help, sewage had seeped under the floating walls (not attached to the foundation) and onto the carpet of the recently finished basement. The clogging culprit was all the way down at the drain by the street. Now that the clog had cleared, I had an even bigger mess to clean up. With a working drain, I easily cleaned up the cement in the utility closet. I also had to call a carpet-cleaning service to do a major water extraction and cleanup. The dry-out took a couple of days while I moved fans to reach all the wet areas. I also paid to have the affected carpet pads replaced to prevent future issues. While some of these problems can be easily avoided, often we must dig deep with a sense of humor and make some phone calls for help.

Each of these examples highlights the need to consider calling in a contractor and paying someone else to do the work. In the last situation, I probably could have rented a machine to do the work, but I would have missed the need to replace the pads underneath the carpet. By calling an expert who had the right tools, I avoided future costly repairs and, potentially, illness.

Similarly, when leading from the middle, we often have to call in experts, or at least coordinate with them. As a leader in the middle of the organization, you have now gained more trust and tend to have more to lose—there's more at risk when you make a mistake. You have more autonomy but not total discretion. You need to know what to share down with your team, what to escalate, and what to handle at your level. And to become an expert on this aspect of leadership, you need to gain enough experience at this level. If you don't stay in the middle long enough, you may miss out on key experiences you'll need as you move up in the organization. The biggest challenge when leading from the middle is knowing when to call in external experts. While it can be beneficial to pay someone else, most larger companies will require you to look within the organization for expertise before escalating the request to the next level.

Depending on your perspective, the journey in the middle can be quite rewarding. Depending on the levels of trust and the culture, it can also be very frustrating. When leading from the middle, you provide the glue. As you build your network, you extend your influence and leadership potential. As you navigate in the middle, you become the one who connects the people, resources, and timing. You need to have the depth of understanding and the breadth to see across the organization. You don't have to know all the information—you just need to remember who else can fill the gaps.

For example, I was on a project where we had to do some building renovations in addition to the technical focus for the project. I needed to have insight into the other schedule dependencies, but I also recognized I had to let the facilities architect manage the building renovation details. We collaborated on key dependencies, so we had a shared vision. Then we communicated often as the project progressed. The closer to the completion and very public launch date, the more detailed the communication. I personally didn't execute the detailed procurements, but I knew the person managing it and ensured that we coordinated or at least checked in on a regular basis. Although it was one of the toughest high-pressure projects I've worked, it was also one of the most rewarding. It has given me an extra boost of confidence later in my career when taking on new projects.

> *You don't have to know all the information— you just need to remember who else can fill the gaps.*

Those of us who thrive in the middle tend to be the mediators, the ones who are comfortable in a roomful of people and plugged in to the details or those with the details. From your vantage point in the middle of the organization, you will often see the opportunities to look within your organization for expertise or pay someone else to save valued resources.

–13–

Leave It for the Next Guy

Know When to Let Go

I f you have ever been caught in a Florida downpour out on a trail, you might see the wisdom in leaving the poop for the next guy or the next time you have an opportunity to pick it up. Sidewalks have also presented a challenge with a stubborn dog that prefers them. While you can often get most of the poop up with the inside-out pickup, further attempts may just put a hole in the bag.

If you live in the big city with pups, you may have stories I can only imagine. I admit that I improvised and did my best with the pickups when on the four-day road trip from Colorado to Florida. We looked for the best places to stop and found that sometimes the midnight stop for the dogs at a rest stop off the highway may not be the safest place to pause with the cell phone light and two dogs for a pickup. I thank all of you in advance for your grace with this admission. I also thank the rest stop landscape company for the assist. In these situations, timing plays a key role in whether we may be willing to chance a fine, a stern look from a neighbor, even the occasional guilty conscience.

I noticed recently that the rake for the pooper-scooper had broken to the point that it shrank from about three and a half feet to one foot. While it still functions, it no longer functions at capacity. It requires extra time and effort to get the same results. The partial rake reminded me of how we can become stagnant in our careers and in our relationships. While we still function well in the organization and produce results, a fresh perspective or new opportunity could prevent long-term painful consequences. Once we make the decision to change to a different position, we find ourselves with many opportunities to let go and leave it for the next guy. From a practical perspective, priorities will also have to change. While we may be capable of performing many tasks ourselves, some tasks may not be beneficial. In the midst of a move, whether across the country, down the street, or down the hall at work, you will have daily choices to take it with you, take the extra time to do it yourself, or leave it for the next guy.

When leaving a position for a new opportunity, you will likely need to trust a vision, idea, process, or team to your successor.

When leaving a position for a new opportunity, you will likely need to trust a vision, idea, process, or team to your successor. In a healthy organization, you have already taken the time to start training your successor well ahead of seeking a new opportunity. No matter how well you have groomed someone to adopt your vision, your successor will likely make changes you had never considered and hopefully will continue building on the legacy. One way to start the process of cross-training prospective successors is to delegate your tasks while you are out of the office on vacation or fulfilling extended travel commitments. If you practice leaving key tasks for your deputy or a trusted individual on your team, both of you will gain a new perspective. The one you left it with comes to understand a portion of your role and has walked a mile in your boots. You now have common ground and potentially new insights into too familiar situations and processes. When you trust others during your vacation, you get the long-overdue break and allow your deputy to exercise his or her leadership skills with the benefit of a safety net through a quick phone call to you if needed.

While I am not trying to replicate the many good books on prioritizing tasks and time management, here are a few tips unique to leading from the middle to help the next leader:

- Provide the background on upcoming key meetings and empower your successor to build the charts and possibly present them *to* you or *for* you before you leave. It will give you the opportunity to introduce the key players in the organization and provide potential discussion points that may arise during the meeting.

- Provide an email or document with links to the locations of key information for future reference. Key information includes recent drafts of charts, documents, schedules, upcoming delivery milestones, and budgets already developed that may provide examples for future tasks. This email or document can also become a time-saver when new members join the team.

- Introduce your team members to key contacts whenever possible and share with the team a little bit about how you know each contact. Then, when a team member receives tasks that may involve a particular contact, whether as your successor or as a colleague who moves on to new opportunities, you have helped him or her with some common ground for relationship building.

–14–

Bring Extra Bags

Anticipate Questions

Since moving to Florida, I started using the poop pickup bags provided at the "poop box." Whether in the neighborhood, the apartment complex, or even at the hotel, the normally provided and restocked bag stations would occasionally come up empty. I have found one totally empty or down to the last few bags. I took what I thought I would need for my two dogs and tried to leave some for the next dog walker. If the empty trend continued, I would purchase my own supply of bags to ensure we could still pick up the poop responsibly. When my dogs had their own yard, they rarely pooped out on a walk. On one instance, my supply was depleted, and I found an empty box at four different bag stations. As we returned from a trip around the retention pond, Cody decided to stop in the front yard of a neighbor's house about ten houses away from ours. What made it so memorable? He left his deposit in their front yard under a tree, right next to the street sign that reminded us to pick up after the pups. With my pockets still empty, I had no choice but to leave it. The next time we walked, I brought my extra supplies and picked it up.

Early in my career in corporate America, I went through a course called Frontline Leadership by Zenger-Miller. At its core, this course taught basic principles and planning questions. I learned to adapt my leadership style to routinely practice the basic principles. What I found most useful in preparing for key meetings were the planning questions. I learned to think about how other people might react to my feedback and to anticipate how I might respond to their responses. By anticipating how others might respond, I also took the time to consider their perspectives. Both activities helped me have more constructive feedback discussions. It also allowed me to guide the discussion back to the focus instead of getting sidetracked by potential deflection and blame games. The training also had us do some role-playing on both sides of the conversation (as the lead and as the team member), which helped us practice and get immediate insights into our blind spots before we had a similar discussion in a real situation.

My extra preparation limited the times I felt blindsided or unprepared during key meetings.

In multiple positions later in my career, I found myself presenting key independent risk evaluation data to directors and vice presidents. One of their key drivers for our organization was to anticipate the questions, identify key risks, and look for mitigation options early. While I brought the perspective of a seasoned technical expert, I also returned to some of those planning questions, even developing some of my own, to anticipate issues and consider other perspectives. Whether or not they had considered the questions I anticipated, or responded how I thought they might, my extra preparation limited the times I felt blindsided or unprepared during key meetings. However, the potential pitfall with anticipating too much is forgetting to listen and being ready to do some rework. While you take the time to prepare and to bring your extra insights, keep an open mind without getting so tied to your approach that you start to resent any feedback that requires rework.

–15–

Gators in the Pond

Lead by Example

s I walked the dogs in my neighborhood, I became aware that we were being watched—not in a creepy way, but I felt the need to stay alert. We have retention ponds in Central Florida, and I am fortunate to live next to a wildlife preserve, which includes one of the largest alligator preserves in Lake Jesup. Our walks often included a gator sighting and always included birds of some sort. Of course, Cody found the perfect spot to poop on the sidewalk right in front of a five-foot gator in the pond. In a case like this, a quiet and quick pickup makes sense depending on your comfort level with looking a gator in the eye. Otherwise, you might consider the leave-it-for-the-next-guy option. I chose to make the inside-out pickup while the dogs distracted the gator. Normally I persuaded the pooches to pick up the pace and keep moving in hopes that they would find a less risky spot.

The birds, from blue herons to night owls, ducks, ospreys, and vultures, all dominated our immediate airspace. I've had hawks and ospreys follow us for over a mile. They would just sit on their perch, watching and waiting.

Similar to the birds and the gators, if you're leading at any level, you'll find out quickly that others will take notice. Someone is always watching and listening. Our actions speak so much louder than anything we can ever say. About fifteen years ago, I became very aware that someday many of the young leaders would be leading our company at the director or vice president level. Some of the young engineers on my team who looked to me for guidance now direct large organizations.

I am a firm believer in leading by example. I tend to avoid asking others on my team to do tasks that I am not willing to try or haven't done myself. One of my best examples of this reluctance was when I was a young lieutenant in the Army Reserve. We went out to the field (civilians might call this structured camping) and had to put up the tents. My training to this point involved setting up one-person pup tents and a family camping tent. However, the larger units had what the supply officer would call the General Purpose (GP) tent that came in small, medium, and large. We had about a dozen women in the unit of about 150 soldiers. One of the sergeants asked me if I knew how to put up the GP small tent for the females. I responded, "No clue. How about I help put up your GP large tent, then you help us with our GP small?" I had been in the unit about four months, and this was my first trip to the field with them. Next thing I knew, I stood underneath the middle of this massive canvas tent, holding up the middle pole while ten other soldiers raised the other inner and outer poles. After we had the whole thing staked off and secured, I emerged, hot, sweaty, and dirty, ready to tackle the next tent. The same sergeant replied as I found him to help with our tent, "You're all right, LT." I found out later that this same sergeant didn't really like officers, and I had changed his perspective.

Later in my career, I had the opportunity to change the perspective of the leaders around me. I love to read both nonfiction and fiction, and I have often shared one leadership book that has had a positive impact on my personal leadership style: *How Full Is Your Bucket?* by Tom Rath and Donald O. Clifton, Ph.D. About fifteen years ago I found it in the grocery store book section one weekend and was sharing it with others within days. It uses the analogy of an invisible bucket and states that every interaction with others either fills their buckets or empties them, one drop at a time, or one interaction at a time.

> Each of us has an invisible bucket. It is constantly emptied or filled, depending on what others say or do to us. When our bucket is full, we feel great. When it's empty, we feel awful.
>
> Each of us also has an invisible dipper. When we use that dipper to fill other people's buckets—by saying or doing things to increase their positive emotions—we also fill

our own bucket. But when we use that dipper to dip from others' buckets—by saying or doing things that decrease their positive emotions—we diminish ourselves.

Like the cup that runneth over, a full bucket gives us a positive outlook and renewed energy. Every drop in that bucket makes us stronger and more optimistic.

But an empty bucket poisons our outlook, saps our energy, and undermines our will. That's why every time someone dips from our bucket, it hurts us.

So we face a choice every moment of every day: We can fill one another's buckets, or we can dip from them. It's an important choice—one that profoundly influences our relationships, productivity, health, and happiness.[4]

As I shared it with other colleagues and leaders at work, I noticed a perspective shift among my peers and leaders as well. Our conversations took on a different tone, and our hallway interactions became more intentional. In almost every mentoring relationship I have entered into since, I have recommended this book. I have had junior engineers find me years later, after they had become the team leaders, and mention how that one perspective shift impacted their interactions with others and their personal leadership styles.

We must embrace that though we may be leading from the middle, our actions and words have the power to influence others. At some point in the last ten years, I realized that I had become one of the senior technical leaders who could quickly fill someone's bucket with a kind word, with an encouraging conversation, or even with noticing someone's initiative. It's a privilege I don't take lightly. I have challenged more than one team to look again at their interactions and consider how full their bucket is.

Depending on your environment and corporate culture, you'll experience different levels of someone watching. From meetings to hallway conversations to off-duty actions, someone is always taking in your example—either to gauge your impact on the organization or to gauge whether to trust you. What we do with that measuring gauge in times of stress and pressure really shapes what it might take to thrive in the situation.

Let's talk about the meetings. Whether I'm leading the meeting or attending the meeting, I prefer to have an agenda when possible. Meetings can consume most of our workday—as a leader in the middle, you may also experience the meeting before the meeting. In my experience, you will receive the majority of your feedback based on how you interact with others in meetings. As the discussion gets more interesting, someone is always looking for a turn to jump in, a turn to talk. In a meeting with your next-level-up leaders, it gets even more interesting. For example, every leader I know has been given feedback to listen more, interrupt less, talk more, or talk less. Regardless of the meeting, when others grow louder, if you can keep your calm and perspective, others will normally follow. If you let the tension and remarks trip your triggers and show visibly, others will likely follow that as well. To keep me grounded, I tend to have someone I trust in the room who will give me honest, constructive feedback. Richard Carlson, Ph.D., said it this way in *Don't Sweat the Small Stuff at Work*:

> I've found two secrets to making virtually any meeting interesting and as productive as it can possibly be. The first thing I do is use the meeting to practice being "present moment oriented." In other words, I attempt to absorb myself in the meeting—not allowing my mind to wander. This deliberate attempt to be focused allows me to get as much value out of the experience as possible. After all, I'm there anyway. I can spend the time wishing I were somewhere else—or I can think about what I'll be doing later. Or, I can practice being truly present, a really good listener....
>
>   The second commitment I have made regarding meetings is to tell myself that I'm going to learn something new from each meeting. So, I listen intently to what is being said, trying to hear something I don't already know. In other words, rather than comparing what I'm hearing to what I already believe—or agreeing or disagreeing in my mind to what is being said—I'm searching for new wisdom, a new insight, or a new way of doing something.[5]

One tactic I have used to avoid interrupting while capturing a fleeting thought is to write it down in my notes. Then, when the discussion settles or someone asks for additional input, I can mention it or choose to talk about it later in a smaller setting or at a more opportune time. My leadership style tends to be expressive and passionate, which can help command a roomful of people; however, it can also scare off a roomful of introverts. While I am a work in progress, I continue to look for ways to improve my communication in all settings. Someone is always

> *Our actions speak loudly. What we say or do gives others permission to say or do the same.*

watching how we react and how we lead. Our actions speak loudly. What we say or do gives others permission to say or do the same.

−16−

Surprising Remedies

Remain Humble

About two weeks after I had settled into the new apartment with the dogs and their "dog park," I had a dog pickup close to an ant bed. I swatted an ant away and gave it little further thought. The next day, I had a blister-looking bump on my index finger. Thinking it was just that, a blister, I popped it and let the fluid get on the skin. Another day later, my finger was swollen and in persistent pain. I took some allergy medicine thinking the swelling was an allergic reaction or a bug bite. When the pain and swelling continued, I decided to get the medical folks at work to check it out. The nurse practitioner asked if I had been near any fire ants. Mystery solved! She took a different route for treatment than I expected. She covered it with medicated bandages that contained antibiotic gel and a pain reliever. It cleared up within a day or two. Practical tip: if you find yourself bitten by a fire ant, go for the antibiotic ointment.

On summer evenings in Florida, frogs of all sizes appear. My Colorado natives lost interest in the lizards quickly, but frogs presented a whole new adventure. Depending on the type of frog, they also presented a danger for the dogs, despite the dogs' fascination with them. Dingo loved to go out at night and look for frogs. Cody had less interest. I grew up in Florida, but I confirmed that I still do not like frogs up close. It's an irrational fear perhaps, but I definitely keep a light handy in case the poop pile starts jumping.

While I saw the occasional snake in Colorado when I was out walking on the trails, I rarely had to deal with them in my yard or up close. Florida has ivy-type bushes that stay close to the ground and grow outward. They are popular around hotel and business parking lots. Cody couldn't resist them and enjoyed walking right through them, sometimes even pooping in them. One morning as he started to walk in the ivy, I noticed a red, yellow, and black snake slithering among the leaves. I squelched my vocal surprise and quickly decided to go another way without incident—or poop. I didn't take the time to determine whether it was the poisonous version or the harmless type. I avoided that route for a few weeks after that. About once a year, we have a snake adventure—either a baby snake in the pool or a larger one slinking around the wild ferns. The babies get thrown over the fence. Thankfully, the rest have left on their own without incident.

One of my most memorable critter cleanups was while we were still in Colorado. One winter evening, Dingo and Cody came running to the door after quite a bit of commotion by the back fence. We had snow on the ground, with another snowstorm headed our way. The bitter cold had the dogs running inside quickly. And then we smelled it. A skunk had sprayed them from the other side of the fence. Fortunately, the skunk was not actually in the yard. It was getting late, and there was little I could do that night about the smell. I put the dogs to bed in their crates and started looking for the next steps. I attempted to ward off some of the smell by putting a new fragrant air filter pad on the furnace filter. I chose the pine scent, thinking it would mask the skunk aroma. In hindsight, I had forgotten that the dog crates were located near the clean air return.

By the next morning, the smell was unbearable. My son bailed to his dad's house, and the dogs went to the vet. The vet provided practical tips for both the dog and house cleanup. While both dogs then went directly to a groomer for a de-skunking session, I returned to the house to begin the deep clean in the house. Despite the snow flurries outside, I opened the windows and pulled out the carpet cleaner and the de-skunking solution to clean the carpets and the furniture. I weathered the cold temperatures and hosed down the dog crates with a healthy dose of de-skunking solution. I cleaned the wood floors and did the laundry. I changed the furnace filter, again. When the dogs returned and the carpets dried, I thought I had overcome most of the smell. I may have just adapted and become immune to it.

A week later, I thought everything had recovered and left on a business trip. While I had washed my clothes to get rid of the skunk smell, I had forgotten to fumigate the suitcase. By the time I opened my suitcase in the hotel room, the odor had returned. After dinner with my colleagues, I went to the grocery store and stocked up on supplies to remedy this smelly situation. I soaked my suitcase in deodorizer and filled it with fabric softener dryer sheets, then left it in the hotel closet with the door closed to limit further exposure. We laughed at a few Pepé Le Pew jokes that week. I also heard every home remedy for skunk cleanup as well as every skunk story on the team. If you live near skunks, I highly recommend that you keep some de-skunking solution on hand and hope you never need to use it.

> *I am learning that humility lets someone else have the better story without diminishing mine.*

If you have ever had to clean up after a skunk encounter or kill a snake, you likely just started retelling and laughing at your own story. You may even have a better story than mine. I am learning that humility lets someone else have the better story without diminishing mine. I grew up with siblings and have a strong competitive streak. From a distance, my confidence can come across as intimidating arrogance. For a long time, I apologized for my strengths (and weaknesses), thinking that my self-deprecating remarks made me humble instead of highlighting my low self-esteem.

Our need to be right or desire to have the best story can undermine the best leaders and destroy trust on your teams. Alternatively, when I can smile and authentically appreciate someone else's story with my undivided attention, then I have become humble. While you will face fierce competition leading from the middle of your organization, you will also have unique opportunities to shine in ways that recognize others for their contributions without diminishing your valued impact.

In every team I lead, we continue to look for ways to improve. We look for new and creative ways to solve a problem. Using rapid brainstorming sessions can yield a bucketful of ideas, especially when you allow the ideas to flow without gauging their viability. We just write them down and keep moving forward. After we capture the ideas, we take another, slower, more deliberate look through them. During this methodical consideration of every idea, we agree as a team on which ones to pursue further and which ones to send to the parking lot or the shredder. We also evaluate each idea on its own merit with an eye on implementation cost and payoff. In the best cases, we find a great idea that will pay huge dividends in savings with a low implementation cost and move forward on them. The costly ones that will yield limited benefit get dropped. Those in the middle get additional attention after further investigation in the cost-benefit trade-off. Implementing these methods brings creative problem-solving to the team and provides the best payoff.

Our need to be right or desire to have the best story can undermine the best leaders and destroy trust on your teams.

–17–

"It Wasn't Me!"

Use Your Gifts in a New Way

We have all experienced times when we've smelled something and started looking for the dog. The dog, of course, either looks at us proudly or shrugs as if to say, "It wasn't me!" It reminds me of the time my daughter decided to try out a new recipe to make a chocolate chip cookie in a mug. If you haven't tried one of these, it can be a quick, hot, gooey cookie, perfect for topping with ice cream as a late-night snack. On this particular evening, she made the cookies that only required the egg yolks. I saw the two egg whites, and I remembered my grandmother used to make meringue by whipping egg whites. I pulled out the small hand whisk and started stirring vigorously. After about two minutes, while the cookies cooked in the microwave oven, I decided my egg-white concoction needed some sugar to stiffen up. Two or three more minutes into this little science project, and I thought, "This is a fail." I looked up at my daughter and said, "I wonder what would happen if we nuked them." My daughter already thought I was a little off with this one. I proceeded to pop the semi-whipped egg whites with sugar in them into the microwave.

Within thirty seconds, we looked at each other, covered our noses, and saw Dingo and Cody come in the kitchen. They took one sniff and ran the other way. I had unknowingly created the perfect stink bomb! Oh, it smelled awful. We laughed until we cried. Then we quickly opened the doors and windows and went searching for the air freshener. I think we finally just threw away the plastic container with the offending smell in the garage. We laughed even more every time we saw the dogs with that look that said, "It wasn't me!"

Sometimes we take a chance and try something new and different, and it turns out just like that stink bomb. Clearly the meringue experiment could have turned into something tasty had I taken a little more time to research the right way to make it. With the right perspective, we can keep learning.

I started learning this lesson in the swimming pool at a young age. I love to swim. My father noticed a natural talent after I spent a couple of summers at the neighborhood pool. He thought I might enjoy the challenge of competitive swimming when I was seven. I was definitely in my element and spent just about every summer in the pool improving my technique and working on my endurance. I learned the value of pacing, of saving some for the end of the race to finish strong. I excelled at the individual medley, the butterfly, and the breaststroke, especially in the middle-distance races. I loved to go fast, improved my times, and won enough to want to continue. One summer, when I was ten, I spent six weeks at camp in North Carolina. I had to learn new skills in the pool, such as treading water and new strokes, including the sidestroke, to gain the Red Cross badges and pass swimming class. In high school, the swimming coach introduced us to water polo to keep us in shape in the off-season. As the goalie, I returned to my treading water and sidestroke (scissor) kicks to defend the goal, up high in the water. We also added *head-up* swimming to "dribble" the ball up and down the pool. Both of these improved my overall skills in the pool.

At NMMI, I expanded my swimming knowledge further as an assistant coach to the high school swim team. In this role, I taught others what I had already learned while I continued to learn from the head coach. The head coach also convinced me to take his water safety instructor course. Once again, I found another use for my *head-up* swimming, treading water, and sidestroke. On a rescue, you had to jump feet first, pop up quickly, and swim with your head up to keep your eyes on the victim. In the best of cases, you just assisted the victims, flipped them on their backs, and pulled them in using the sidestroke. In the worst of cases, you had to dive down and pull the victims up to the surface before assisting them using the sidestroke. The next year, I took kayaking and learned more water skills, including sculling. We used sculling to bodysurf feet first down sections of the Rio Grande river. I still treasure the times I spent as a lifeguard during my second year at NMMI and the Bottomless Lakes triathlon, as well as the summer I spent as a lifeguard and teaching swim classes in Clearwater. During my second semester at Florida State, I joined the synchronized swimming club. The coach loved my technique and expanded my sculling skills. Synchronized swimming required another focus—it focused on endurance and poise, timing over speed, sculling to move into new positions, and treading water to create different effects. Once again, I learned new skills to augment my already deep knowledge and love of the water. A few years later, I had the opportunity to coach a youth swim team in Germany and even took a few swimmers to the youth national championships.

If we can look at the problem in a different way, we may find doors open to us when we apply our talents and strengths in a new way.

I use those examples to show how the coach continued to build on skills I already had but was using in a different way. Technical leadership in the software industry reminds me of the swimming skills examples. I gained the initial skills with a degree in computer science, then continued to add depth and breadth by building on skills and talents I already possessed. I just applied them in different ways. If we can look at the problem in a different way, we may find doors open to us when we apply our talents and strengths in a new way. While I have enjoyed some projects more than others, every one of them prepared me for the next season, the next challenge, the next adventure.

Like with the science project, setbacks and burnout may cause us to run in the other direction, saying, "It wasn't me!" However, sometimes we have to take a risk and step out of our comfort zone and learn something new using our gifts and talents in a new way.

–18–

Rain or Shine

Keep Showing Up!

I have enjoyed the unconditional love of dogs for most of my life. I love their attention and comfort. Their uncontainable joy can make me laugh on the worst of days. Their unconditional love has greeted my children and me as we've returned home from a long day or even a short trip to the store. They love to join us on most adventures. They also rely on us for their meals, exercise, training, and visits for waste management. Rain or shine, the dogs need someone to show up for them.

The summer I spent in an apartment and then a hotel room with two dogs had more than the usual summer tropical storms. Though the storm was not as destructive as some later hurricane seasons, the dogs and I weathered our first tropical storm within two weeks of our arrival in Florida. The week of the first tropical storm's arrival also brought destructive fires across the state of Colorado and into my home of twenty years in Colorado Springs. The dogs had experienced stormy weather in Colorado but rarely with full days of heavy rain and thunderstorms. Three or four times a day, I would look for lulls in the rain to get the pooches out to do their business. They would stay close to me, attempting to remain under the umbrella, and do their business quickly.

Two months later in the hotel, we experienced three different tropical storms during our forty-five-day stay. I recall watching the weather and rushing back from work at lunchtime to get their longer walk in during the nice weather and glimpse of sunshine. We would then persevere through evenings of persistent downpours and quick trips down four flights of stairs with the umbrella or rain jacket. A few nights in the hotel included midnight wake-ups with an urgent message of "Gotta go now!" In your own home, you get up and stand on the porch while the dogs go out in the rain, but in a hotel, you have to get up, get shorts and shoes on, get the leash, and go out with them.

On other days, we would leave the comfort of the air-conditioned room and venture out on hot days, on hot pavement, and into instant moisture. In the high heat, we had to be careful to keep the pooches off the hot sidewalks and pavement and stick to the shady routes in the grass. On most days, we enjoyed the early morning and late evening walks before the traffic noise and before the mosquitoes came out. Both dogs became better at understanding "last out."

Fast-forward a few years, and I am riding out Hurricane Irma from the laundry room with two dogs and an old clock radio that took batteries. After the hurricane prep and the tornado warnings, we were happy to hide out in that room. If you have ever dealt with a hurricane off the coast, you know you hear the warnings, get the data, and start preparing. The grocery stores are packed full of people as everyone starts shopping for nonperishables and munchies, and the supplies dwindle, emptying the aisles.

I went through hurricanes as a child and really never thought about the preparations required. Based on our experience with Hurricane Michael the year before, we made adjustments to our preparations and supplies. You start to look at everything through a new lens. When they say hunker down, you look for anything and everything that could become a projectile given enough wind force, and then you move it into the house or garage. The inside prep becomes a challenge too. You look at the enclosed spaces in the middle of the house without windows. In our case, it was a small closet under the stairs, the laundry room, and for a small time the bathroom. Our initial plan was for all of us to hide out in this small closet. Of course, the closet was full of boxes and other stuff, which we then moved into the study, a bedroom on the first floor with only one window on the south side, away from the road. As the rain continued that day, we noticed a short break in the downpour in the afternoon and decided to take the dogs on a short walk for a last out to calm them. I put on the heartiest rain jacket I could find in the house (bright green), my daughter's rubber polka-dot rain boots, and my favorite FSU hat. The dogs and I were ready. We had hunkered down the doors at the front with sandbags and blocked off the garage door, so we made our way out the back fence. The rain totally stopped as soon as we hit the sidewalk. We enjoyed a short walk with a couple of pickups and returned relatively dry. Then the wind picked up as the sky darkened again.

With the first tornado warning, we gathered our munchies, added comfy cushions to the closet, brought the radio and cell phones, and piled into the closet with the dogs. After about three minutes and a photo opportunity, we all agreed our plan needed an update, and quick! My daughter kept the closet since she had prepared that space. My son started in the bathroom and after about five minutes decided to chance it in the study, which had a window. I ended up in the laundry room with the radio and the dogs on a couple of futon cushions. We spent the night in these positions due to the sixty- to seventy-mile-per-hour winds howling outside. We would check in every few hours after another tornado warning alerted us. We emerged safe in the morning to minimal damage, clear skies (if only for a few hours), no power, and then more rain—but thankfully no flooding.

Our power was out for four days. I stayed home with the pooches, as they were now seniors that moved a bit slower. I bought a spray bottle to mist them often to keep them cool. We also took a few rides in the air-conditioned car to get ice cream for the dogs and cool off. After three nights in the heat and powerless house, we decided to spend a night in a hotel that had power. So the dogs and I returned to that same hotel we lived in for forty-five days years before. We spent a peaceful, cool night as the power returned at home. I know our experience was relatively mild compared with many who have weathered hurricanes with devastating power and destruction.

In leadership, in life, we will experience rainy days. We will experience hot, sticky sunny days as well. During bitter-cold blizzards and rainy days, we long for sunshine. After weeks, months, or even years of drought, with no rain in sight, we long for easy rainy days inside. One day at a time, leaders keep showing up. At any level, leaders emerge with perseverance in the storms.

Teams look to their leaders on their bad days for their encouragement, for their "don't quit" attitudes. Senior leaders look to the middle of the organization to stay the course, to keep the teams moving toward the goal—toward the short-term goals with an eye on the long-term vision. As leaders, we must be dependable and accountable. Taking ownership of the plan may look different depending on the long-term vision and culture of the organization. In times of extreme schedule pressure, we often find the most creative solutions. I have developed quite a few schedules for large-scale, very visible projects. At the beginning of the project, we have the most optimism. Many people have written books on how to schedule a large project. In my experience, a good plan considers the dependencies, the unknowns, and the prior performance. It also anticipates the delays and builds in margin. A great plan includes risk mitigations and off-ramps and identifies opportunities. Opportunities come when we anticipate issues and mitigate them early, when we look at efficiencies where

> *At any level, leaders emerge with perseverance in the storms.*

we can work tasks in parallel, or when we see the need to add more people. Any plan requires diligence and consistent performance. As leaders, we anticipate and manage the dependencies to keep the team performing and moving forward. We remove the obstacles before they arrive.

In all cases, we make progress one task, one day at a time. We ask the tough questions, such as, "How do we know we're done?" However, not all schedule pressures can be overcome with more people. I have seen "no kidding" schedule problems that required a different approach. For example, in the simplest terms, loading software depends on the arrival and availability of the hardware. We often focus on the software availability. In the middle of a major technical refresh project, as we came down to the last three months of the project, we almost overlooked the hardware dependency. We quickly started looking again at the off-ramps and contingency plans. Almost daily until the final checkout, we looked at new contingency plans, just in case. When you get into those scenarios, even the most off-the-wall, seemingly too expensive, "They'll never go for it" ideas come into play.

I once asked my team of engineers to describe attributes of a leader using two words, without repeating what others already said. What a formidable list! I really enjoyed that exercise because within about ten minutes, junior engineers shared their expectations for their current leadership. At the same time, the whole team benefited from the wisdom of the more seasoned engineers on the team. As you look over this list, I challenge you to look for yourself, add to the list, add your own personal style, and identify some traits you want to grow:

- Good listener
- Friendly
- Encouraging
- What happened?
- Brings donuts
- Reliable, accessible
- Open-minded
- Multifaceted background
- Unselfish, dedicated
- Situational awareness
- Trustworthy
- Guileless
- Resilient, adaptable
- Defends subordinates
- Smiles under pressure
- By example
- Timely
- Calming presence
- Invisible
- Enables people
- Force multiplier
- Well thought of
- Fearless
- Inclusive
- Command presence
- Thick-skinned
- Unbounded optimism
- Helpful
- Accountable
- Personality
- Responsible
- Effective communicator
- Omniscient
- Paying overtime
- Common sense
- Transparent
- Free candy
- Nice, empowering
- Unnecessarily quarrelsome
- Lead, follow
- Wise
- Non-crabby

I could have deleted some of these, but each one represents an individual person, at a key point in time, with a unique perspective on leadership. Some had more profound insights than others. Some went with humor and practical answers. All of them shared their thoughts and feedback. Whether or not we want to acknowledge it, all of us might feel like that "What happened?" style after a meeting with senior leadership. On those "What just happened?" days, we need to show up. I can recall that on some of my darkest days while in survival mode, when I was asked, "How are you doing?" I answered, "I showed up." As leaders, we may not always appreciate the strength and perseverance it takes to just show up.

In the spring of 2019, Dingo became sick the day before I was due home from a business trip. I changed my schedule and did my best to arrive home earlier than planned, to show up for him. I had one more full day with my faithful friend before we had to take him and let him go. His body was filled with tumors, and he had lost the will to eat. At fourteen years old, we had to say good-bye. Cody continued to enjoy a few more weeks. As he struggled to walk, we helped him out to the yard. As he began falling more and more often and lost interest in food, we had to let him go as well. These are tough days and tough decisions—tough times to keep showing up. It is so difficult to balance our need to have them with us with their ability to thrive without pain. Their wonderful personalities could never be replaced. However, the silence without them didn't last long. Before we knew it, we had rescued Oscar and added little Winnie, who continue to teach us new things and need us to show up, rain or shine, to pick up the poop.

As a final thought on leading from the middle, consider what it looks like from the middle lane on the highway. As we move down the middle lane in our own careers, some will pass us quickly on the left with help from mentors, a great job and skills match, and accelerated promotions. Others may lag behind us in the right lane, finding their own pace through leadership challenges, maybe choosing to stay more technical a little longer. Others may pull off the road and choose to do something totally different, taking another path with a fresh start. Only you can decide your pace, your path, and your destination. You have a choice to jump into the fast lane and accelerate your leadership opportunities. You also have a

> *You have a choice to jump into the fast lane and accelerate your leadership opportunities.*

choice to slow things down and take a less hasty pace. Whatever the pace or the route, I hope you will embrace your time in the middle lane, including both the startups and the setbacks. If you find yourself stalled, pull over, refuel, and reset your course for the next adventure. Find your unique leadership style and thrive in your environment.

Acknowledgements

My sincere thank you to everyone who took the time to listen to my stories and encourage me to write this book. Many of you will recognize yourselves in the retelling of the story. Thank you in advance for your grace with any oversights or missed details. I have intentionally left out your names (for your protection and mine) so that the next generation may also recognize themselves in similar situations.

I also want to thank the many leaders who have invested in me, challenged, and trusted me with their projects throughout my career. To members of my teams—it takes the whole team to make it work—I hope you also learned as many lessons as I have.

I'm grateful for every mentoring conversation—every one of them contributed leadership nuggets. Thank you to the many coaches, both in sports and in life, who saw potential and spent time growing my skills and perspective. A special hug and heartfelt thank you to those who walked me through the dark days. Your kind words and extra attention remind me how to help others as they walk through their dark days. I hope that you see the impact of our simple conversations.

To my early reviewers, your encouraging feedback and insights provided the helpful nudge to finish well. I couldn't have done it without you.

Thank you to David and Caroline at Higher Life Publishing for seeing my potential and having the patience to let this one "simmer a while" during a pandemic. Also thank you to Melissa for your unique perspective during the content editing—any editing escapes are all mine. I appreciate the efforts of the entire team to work through design updates and schedule changes.

To those who have always known me as "Bunker," you may never know the impact you've had on my life. I cherish every adventure.

To my daughter, Chelsea, and my son, CJ, I sincerely appreciate your patience and support through this journey. I hope that these insights and nuggets will help you along the way as you navigate your own paths.

Finally, I give all of the credit, honor, and glory to Jesus Christ, my Lord and Savior. Thank you for this assignment—may it serve You well.

Endnotes

Preface: Leading from the Middle

[1]Dr. Kevin Leman, *The Birth Order Book: Why You Are the Way You Are* (Ada, MI: Revell, 2009), 152–153, https://www.amazon.com/Birth-Order-Book-Why-You/dp/0800734068.

Chapter 4: Throw It Away

[2]Pippa Mattinson, "Dog Poop Disposal—Where Do You Put Yours?," The Labrador Site, December 3, 2017, http://thelabradorsite.com/dog-poop-disposal.

[3]John C. Maxwell, *Leadershift* (New York: HarperCollins, 2019), 7, 10–11, https://www.google.com/books/edition/Leadershift/t3tgDwAAQBAJ?hl=en&gbpv=1&d-q=leadershift&printsec=frontcover.

Chapter 15: Gators in the Pond

[4]Tom Rath and Donald O. Clifton, PhD, *How Full Is Your Bucket?* (New York: Gallup Press, 2005), 5, https://tinyurl.com/ycds2o5c.

[5]Richard Carlson, *Don't Sweat the Small Stuff at Work* (New York: Hyperion, 1998), 23–24, https://www.amazon.com/Dont-Sweat-Small-Stuff-Work/dp/0786883367.

IF YOU'RE A FAN OF THIS BOOK, WILL YOU HELP ME SPREAD THE WORD?

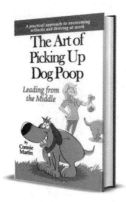

There are several ways you can help me get the word out about the message of this book…

- Post a 5-Star review on Amazon.
- Write about the book on your Facebook, Twitter, Instagram, LinkedIn, – any social media you regularly use!
- If you blog, consider referencing the book, or publishing an excerpt from the book with a link back to my website. You have my permission to do this as long as you provide proper credit and backlinks.
- Recommend the book to friends – word-of-mouth is still the most effective form of advertising.
- Purchase additional copies to give away as gifts.

You can find additional resources and connect with me at www.wordsfromthemeander.com.